# Table of Contents

Introduction ..................................................................................................................................3

Chapter One ................................................................................................................................6

    Keys To Business Success ......................................................................................................6

Chapter Two ..............................................................................................................................10

    Getting Started .....................................................................................................................10

Chapter Three ............................................................................................................................22

    Jewish Wisdom Business Success .......................................................................................22

Chapter Four .............................................................................................................................26

    Make The Most Of The Customers You Have ...................................................................26

# Introduction

Customer management, also known as customer relationship management, has evolved rapidly in 25 years. It started as a combination of database/direct marketing, account management and customer service. Still, it is now a broad and deep discipline – covering a range of topics from customer interaction systems and the databases that support them through customer experience management to advanced quasi-psychological approaches.

Much academic research into the area has focused on customers' willingness to form relationships with suppliers and the latter's attempts to create relationships and exploit them to retain customers, selling more to them and generating more profit from them. However, most academic and practical writing about customer management is relatively weakly connected with thinking about marketing strategy. Examples of poorly integrated marketing thinking include the following:

The assumption that customer retention is always a higher priority than customer acquisition.

The assumption that most customers in most markets are happy to form relationships with brands or companies. Misguided attempts to create relationships with and loyalty by customers who resist the attempt. Over-optimistic forecasts of cross-selling ratios simply because the customer already buys a company's product.

Over-investment in achieving high levels of service for customers of little value. Over-promotion to acquire new customers to achieve customer number targets when the quality of customers being acquired is not good. Acquiring customers and then neglecting them at the critical early stage of the relationship. The independent allocation of acquisition (win), retention (keep) and development budgets.

**The Importance Of Clarity And Simplicity**

Simple put, many companies don't see the wood for the trees. They over-engineer the details of their customer management without getting their strategies right. Others are at the other end of the spectrum – they either have no customer management strategy or have too many. Based on our commercial practice and our research, our view is that companies that perform best in customer management understand that there are four interlocking strategies and 16 supporting sub-strategies for improving customer management – though they may not articulate them precisely as we do. These strategies to a particular company depending on market position, performance, ambition, and attitude to risk. This article briefly explains the strategies and gives examples of how they can be deployed.

**The Four Strategies**

The strategies are as follows:

Winning customers: customer acquisition and activation

Keeping customers: customer retention and maintenance

Developing customers: customer penetration/share of wallet, improving the gross value produced by customers

Efficiency in customer management: reducing cost and increasing yield Each strategy should be assessed against, typically, these four areas:

Impact on the customer – image, advocacy, engagement, satisfaction, social media commentary. Impact on the business – For example, net present value, the trajectory of benefit over time, cash flow, capital investment requirement, operating cost, the opportunity cost of not doing.

Probability of achieving – risk, taking into account the company's culture and history of success and failure in implementing change projects, likely competitor reaction and finally, what knowledge the company has about whether customer behaviour is likely to change as predicted (this element of risk is reduced through piloting and testing).

Compatibility – For example, fit with brand values and image.

There's strength in being strong enough to admit your weaknesses. After all, we all have areas in which we excel and others to use a little work. If you can commit to personal growth to strengthen your weaknesses, it can make you a more well-rounded individual and more diligent worker. This can have incredible effects on your career.

To be clear, working on strengthening your weaknesses doesn't mean you're pursuing perfection, nor does it require undue self-criticism. Instead, it's a challenge that entrepreneurs can embrace a productive self-improvement project that will help them overcome bad habits or tendencies that could hold them back from reaching their full potential.

# Chapter One

# Keys To Business Success

The 21st century is a tumultuous time to be in business. With the rapid rate of technological change, evolving political and economic situations, many business owners find it difficult to operate and survive in the current environment. This is large because the rules that businesses operate on in the 21st century is different to the way it was in the past. Here are the key elements necessary for businesses to succeed in the 21st century:

## Innovation

In the 21st century, innovation is the cornerstone of the success of any business. With constant and never before changes in the business environment, driven by technology and uncertain political and economic situations, innovation is more important than ever before. Only through constant innovation can a business not only survive the current uncertain times but also thrive. Businesses of the 21st century can only drive business growth by systematically embedding innovation into business culture, management practices, and decision making systems.

The consequence of a lack of innovation is strikingly apparent through businesses like Nokia, Blackberry, Yahoo, and Barns and Noble. The simple fact of the matter is, if you do not innovate and stay ahead of the curve, you will end up being left behind. This is as applicable to Fortune 500 companies as it is too small businesses. For example, lack of adoption of digital marketing can keep your business lagging behind others and make it hard for you to gain customers in an increasingly digital age.

Business owners of the 21st century need to rethink the organization and practices of their businesses and embrace innovative practices in all areas of business. Only through relentless innovation can organizations survive in the digital age.

## Flat Organizational Structure

The flat organizational structure is basically a business structure in which there are few or no levels of management between managers of the business and the staff. Businesses need to be agile and be able to respond to external threats and opportunities quickly to survive in the 21st century. A flat organizational structure allows employees more of a say in the decision-making process. It also increases the time needed to take decisions as there would be fewer levels of bureaucracy. Having a flat organizational structure is also important in motivating employees and attracting talented individuals.

## Experimentation

With new technologies such as the Internet and 3D printing, the cost of prototyping has gone down immensely. This allows businesses to prototype quickly to try to understand areas of improvement. Experimentation culture allows for the business to properly match its product to the needs of the consumers at a little financial burden to the business. It will increase the product's chance of success in the long run. One of the key ideas to come out of the Internet boom is that iteration is good. You need to refrain from trying to do everything right the first time and need to be willing to try and build things quickly and take them to market quickly.

Many successful business people will tell you that they were able to achieve success after conquering their inner fears. From that point on, the road to success was a relatively straight shot.

## Purpose

Purpose, for many businesses, is found in its core values. Every business has its own set of values, which may range from respect to perseverance to courage — or all of the above and more.

Following core values helps guide businesses and leaders alike. Leaders have a better understanding of how to respond and make decisions in and out of a crisis because of these core values.

Further, when a leader leans on company values it helps reassure other team members. Leaders that focus on values and practice them create a domino effect with employees, inspiring them to follow suit. Focus, not fear, guides us out of difficult times and into seeing a light at the end of the tunnel.

## Transparency

The importance of good communication became paramount for leaders to share with others in modern time. What happens in a workplace where there is poor communication? In the absence of good communication, team members may speculate about what is really happening within an organization. Gossip about a worst-case scenario could spread like wildfire — and that scenario isn't based on the truth.

Leaders need to continue practising transparency in the modern age and beyond, especially with distributed teams. This ensures that everyone has the right information no matter where they work and feels engaged with the company.

Transparency does more than help communicates the necessary facts to team members. Arming employees with the facts allow them to feel more confidence, trust and support within the business.

## Accountability

Simply put, leaders must be able to walk the talk. If a company took a stance on issues like social justice or environmental sustainability in this time. Leaders must hold themselves, as well as the businesses, accountable to do the necessary work to fulfil these promises. Otherwise, the loss of consumer trust may be impossible to repair.

## Grit

Grit is sticking with your future, day in, day out, not just for the week, not just for the month, but for years, and working really hard to make that future a reality. Grit is living life like it's a marathon, not a sprint." What sticks out in that paragraph to me, where leaders are concerned, is the notion of sticking with your future for years. A similar comparison may be drawn with the coronavirus pandemic. We are now at the year-mark of the pandemic. Even with vaccine distributions, the world isn't 100% sure when the next normal may begin.

That being said, however, leaders that possess grit or begin to embrace a gritty mindset will be able to develop a growth mindset. This is the belief that the ability to learn is not fixed. Rather, it can change with effort. Leaders that make it their mission to strive for grit will ultimately grow from the struggle. They will learn how to adapt when things don't go their way. Grit gives us the inner will to do and the desire to be the best that we can.

Again, this has a domino effect to the benefit of a leader. Grit pushes you to achieve new goals, try new things, create new boundaries, and explore new horizons. Leaders, listen up. Start putting all of these qualities in action for a better year that allows us to be the best versions of ourselves.

# Chapter Two

# Getting Started

People generally start a small business or buy a small business for different reasons. Sometimes it is because they are good at their chosen profession and feel that they can make a better living working for themselves, sometimes it is a lifestyle change and sometimes it is simply a lifelong dream.

With the advent of retrenchment and redundancy pack-ages or early retirement payouts there are many more people facing retirement long before they are actually ready. They have cash and they have the energy and enthusiasm to start their own business. The problem is that they rarely have the experience required to run their new venture and to make money.

**Does your business stand out from the crowd?**

Standing out from the crowd is important and it really is one of the main fundamentals of any marketing strategy. These days people have a lot of choice. With the advent of the Internet that choice has increased even more. If people can't find your number easily or if you are hidden away among your competitors you may be in trouble. It is important to send out a very clear message that you are here, you are ready, willing and able to be of service and most importantly of all that you are great at what you do. There are various ways to increase your chances of standing out from the crowd and these ideas are detailed in this section:

- Promote your business from the outsid
- Put your message on the company car
- Turn your invoice into a sales tool
- Sell yourself even when you're not there
- Use the Internet to be noticed
- A good uniform impresses everyone
- Make the most of packaging
- Never underestimate the importance of a business card

- Does your business have a memorable name?

## Promote Your Business From The Outside In

Be proud to promote your business by putting a sign on the wall. I used to deal with a large graphic design company that had an upstairs office on one of the busiest intersections in town. They had a huge wall in full view from anywhere on the intersection and they never got around to painting a sign on this wall. Eventually they moved out because business was bad. If they had spent a few hundred dollars on a simple sign business would have got a whole lot better a whole lot faster.

Outdoor signage works seven days a week, 24 hours a day, whether you are open or closed. Use it to its full advantage. Be aware of local government regulations govern-ing signage restrictions such as size. Work with these regulations but make your signs as big as you legally can. Don't clutter them, just a few words outlining what you do and when you are open. Make the colours stand out and check any artwork thoroughly for spelling or grammat-ical mistakes.

## Put Your Message On The Company Car

Like all outdoor signage, company vehicles are an excellent way to promote your business. Most businesses have at least one company vehicle that can be anything from a utility to a bus. These vehicles tend to be on the road all day, all over the city. What better way to tell people about your business than a moving sign?

Sign-writing on vehicles can be expensive; however, like all advertising, do it to suit your budget. Perhaps start with a set of magnetic signs for the doors and then work your way up to a full paint job.

There are a few key points to remember with any form of moving advertising—keep words to a minimum, make it easy to read and tell people where they can find you and when you are open.

Many companies have overcome this by putting the Yellow Pages sticker on their vehicle. This works well as long as your company is easy to find in the Yellow Pages. If it isn't it should be. Don't make it hard for customers to find you.

A few words of warning with sign-writing on vehicles— you get what you pay for so make sure that the sign-writer gives you a few samples of the work that they have done previously before committing yourself.

I used to have a business partner who was probably the world's worst driver. He was fast, aggressive and all over the road. This was bad enough in his car but when he was in the company vehicle I would receive phone call after phone call from angry motorists abusing me because of the way this maniac was driving. Every time my partner took the car on the road we lost customers. The point here is to make certain that anyone driving your company vehicle is aware that if your name is on the side they are representing your business and should drive safely and courteously.

## Turn Your Invoice Into A Sales Tool

Most companies send out invoices and statements on a regular basis. Invoices are normally passed through a number of hands before they actually reach the person that signs the cheque. This provides the opportunity for you to promote your business to a number of people who are already aware of what you basically do but perhaps not of every facet of what your business has to offer.

This is what we call a 'soft sell' or 'positive reinforce-ment' of your company message. Perhaps you are going to stock a new range or product, perhaps pricing has changed, or your trading hours are different or you simply want to reinforce the strong corporate message that you are already putting across.

A computer software company I dealt with used their company invoice to introduce a new member of staff every month. For example, January's invoice had a picture of Bill Higgins, Sales Manager, with a brief outline of his career history and what role he played in the company. This gave a very personal feel to their business and increased my level of awareness regarding the people that I was dealing with.

The introduction of a company staff member also took the emphasis off the invoice being a bill and I am sure that I paid these accounts much quicker because they had a very personal feel to them. I also felt as if I was a part of that company, a valued customer being shown the inner work-ings of a successful business.

## Sell Yourself Even When You're Not There

Everybody hates being put on hold but unfortunately it is a way of life. If you have the technology to play hold music you can probably arrange to have a company message playing. This is an opportune time to let potential custom-ers know more about your company and the services that you offer.

There are plenty of companies that arrange 'messages on hold' and the cost is not overly expensive. Like most of these marketing ideas it is more a matter of someone making the time to find the company that produces 'mes-sages on hold' and then actually arranging for the service to be installed. This type of marketing produces a very good corporate image and many small companies give the appearance of being a large company by having a profes-sional on hold message.

## Use The Internet To Be Noticed

The Internet is a new and exciting resource that has enormous potential. Advertising on the Internet is a new concept that many businesses don't really understand. I per-sonally look at the Internet like a big library. You know that all of the information is there; it's just a matter of finding it. The amount of information available is virtually beyond comprehension but the key to success is making it easy for people to find your business or product.

Basically there are two ways to promote your business on the Internet. The first is that you can have your own website where people surfing the net may come across your site and decide that they want more information or that they would like to purchase what you are selling. Setting up your own site is becoming cheaper every day and within a couple of years the majority of businesses will have their own websites. Websites can easily be linked to other sites, making it easier for you to be found.

There are companies available that sell fully designed and very impressive websites that you purchase. They simply fill in the blanks and put your company name and your products and services in the right place. So for a few hundred dollars you can have a very professional website up and running. To find these companies search for 'web-site hosting, web design and domain names' on the Inter-net. Many of the companies that offer this service advertise heavily on search engine sites.

The second way to promote your business on the Internet is to purchase what are known as banner adver-tisements. This is where you put an advertisement on someone else's website. The advantage of this is simply that you can promote your business on a highly successful site that is established and perhaps getting hundreds of thou-sands of 'hits' per month.

## A Good Uniform Impresses Everyone

An interesting phenomenon happens when you put a person in a uniform—generally they are treated with more respect because it looks like they have some form of author-ity. This is one of the main reasons why the military and the police dress in uniforms.

Imagine if an airline pilot strolled through the cabin in a Disneyland T-shirt and shorts—how much confidence would this instil in passengers? I would hazard a guess and say not much. In fact, if I was on that particular flight I would be out the door in a second.

If you and your staff are not well presented in smart and practical uniforms maybe you are not sending the right message to your customers. Uniforms tend to be costly but, like

most marketing tools, you purchase them to suit your budget. Perhaps you can start with matching shirts and name tags and work up to skirts, trousers and shorts. Quite often staff will be prepared to pay some of the costs towards their uniforms because it saves them the problem and expense of continually buying new clothes for work.

Once again, find a company uniform that you like and see if you can apply it to your business. Even very small businesses can have a uniform—the size of the business is irrelevant. Once a uniform is established make certain that everyone is clear about how they are expected to wear it. The better presented you and your staff appear the more professional your business will appear. This will instil con-fidence and security in customers when they use your services.

There are shops that specialise in selling uniforms and accessories. They can be found in the Yellow Pages tele-phone directory.

## Make The Most Of Packaging

Many businesses provide packaging for their products. This may be something as simple as a cheap plastic bag right through to an enormous wooden crate. Packaging provides the perfect opportunity for with a company message to be passed on to potential customers that see the packaging as well as to the customer receiving the package. If you are providing the packaging anyway why not use it to increase your sales. Print a company slogan on your wrapping paper, perhaps your trading hours, gift suggestions, new products, change of address information or any other message that you can think of.

Another easy idea that is very rarely used is to slip in a promotional flyer when packaging up an item. If a person has bought something from your business there is a good chance that they will buy something else in the future or perhaps recommend you to a friend.

Book stores are one of the few industries that really take advantage of the potential of in-packaging promotions. Most will include a flyer covering specials of the month, latest releases and special interest type publications as well as giving you a free bookmark promoting the latest release.

## Never Underestimate The Importance Of A Business Card

Business cards are often considered a necessary evil rather than a fantastic marketing tool. Potential customers deduce a lot from your appearance and that of your business card. Make the effort and use your business card to its full potential.

Business cards are normally printed in sheets, which means that you can have a number of different messages or names. By all means use some for names but use the others as mini brochures. Putting your services on the backof a business card only adds marginally to the produc-tion cost but it enhances your card and makes it a very effective tool.

Another option is to have 'bring this card in and receive the following . . .' on your business card. Coffee shops seem to have adopted this idea on mass with virtually every cafe offering a coffee card where you pay for so many cups and you get one free. The business card is your progress record, which is crossed off each time you make a purchase.

This concept works well with restaurants that offer either a free glass of wine with a meal or a free dessert with dinner. The offer is printed on the back of the card and to redeem it the customer must produce the card when dining.

There are many businesses that could use this concept to easily increase the amount of business they are receiving from both new and existing customers.

Once you have fully utilised your business cards the next important step is to distribute them everywhere. The price difference between printing 2000 and 3000 business cards is, once again, quite small—the more you print, the cheaper they become. Put them on noticeboards, in letterboxes, in a stand on your counter, give them to your suppliers, mail them out or stand on a street corner handing them out.

## Do You Make The Most Of The Customers You Already Have?

It is cheaper to keep existing customers than it is to find new ones. Successful businesses work very hard at building solid relationships with their customers. They reward them for shopping regularly, they ask for feedback, they look for ways to constantly improve both the products and the services they are offering. They also never take their customers for granted. The best way to look after existing customers is to stay in touch with them. If you haven't done this in the past, don't worry, it is never too late to send someone a letter to say thank you for their business.

The ideas we'll talk about in this section are:

- Send out reminder notices
- Stay in touch with your customers
- Remember important dates
- Ask your customers for referrals
- Say thank you to generate more business
- What is a loyalty program and can you use one?

## Send Out Reminder Notices

This marketing initiative seems to have only been utilised by dentists, optometrists, the blood bank and vets. When-ever you (or your pets) are due for a check-up you receive a gentle reminder in the mail. What a great idea.

So why doesn't your mechanic send out reminder notices—'Hey, it's been six months since your last service, you better bring the car in'. Or perhaps your solicitor—'It's been two years since we have seen you, perhaps it's time to make a new will'.

This type of mail-out or phone call can bring great results and really all it takes is for you to have records of your clients. It is a gentle, no pressure reminder and a call to action. One dentist I know even goes so far as to schedule an appointment for the clients, letting them know that they will be in touch to confirm the appointment one week prior.

Imagine if every six months a letter turned up smelling of perfume. Out of curiosity you open it and inside is a scented Christmas tree—the type that deodorise your car. Attached is a brief note from your mechanic saying, 'It's been six months since we saw you so your Christmas tree probably needs changing—just like your oil. Joe from our service department will call you in a few days to see if you would like to arrange a convenient time for a service.' One Christmas tree deodoriser and postage will come to about $3.50. I have never had a car serviced for under $100 (normally double this amount), so for a $3.50 invest-ment you are probably going to make a $100 sale—sounds like good business to me.

A stationery company that I buy laser printer refills from knows that I use a cartridge every three to four weeks. Without fail I get a phone call during the third week of the month, asking me if I need another cartridge. I find this very convenient and I am never faced with the dilemma of running out of toner on a Saturday afternoon when I am in the middle of printing out a 300 page document.

Deep down I also like the fact that this company considers me important enough to track my consumer habits. It is also one less thing for me to worry about on a day-to-day

## Stay In Touch With Your Customers

I was recently approached by a small aluminium manu-facturing company. They were having a difficult time as their particular industry had become very competitive in the last few years. After a few minutes of discussing what the main problem was (not enough customers) I asked how long had they been in business. My jaw dropped when they said almost twenty years and during that time they had almost 20 000 customers.

After probing for a few more details it became apparent that once a job was finished and delivered this business had no further contact with the customer. There was no follow-up or after-sales service. Sitting on the floor in some dusty corner was a box filled with the names of thousands of customers that had already used this business but had never

been followed up. This is a very common fault of small business operators. They don't stay in touch with their past customers because they don't know what to say.

The main product that the company offered was the selling and installation of garage doors. It appeared logical that they should offer a free after-sales service call where they visit the house to oil the door, tension the chain and generally make sure that everything is working well. This provides two opportunities. First, the customer feels good because the level of service they have received is great and they will tell their friends. The second opportunity is that the service person representing the company can cas-ually outline the other services and products available, hopefully making another sale.

If you have boxes of past client files laying in a dusty corner, dig them out and get to work immediately. First of all start communication with them. Drop them a line and ask how your product is holding up. Let them know that you will be sending updates about new and exciting prod-ucts and services in the future. These people have already walked through your door once. Assuming they were happy with your business, what is going to stop them from coming back again? Organise the records, check the addresses, phone numbers etc. and make sure that they are up to date and then get started.

Your best source of business could be tucked away in the garden shed under a stack of National Geographic magazines and old

## Remember Important Dates

You can show your existing customers that you are inter-ested in them by remembering important dates such as birthdays and anniversaries. This is the perfect opportunity for you to drop them a line to say congratulations and thank them for their business.

Find out your customers' birthdays by doing a brief survey. If you have a club of some sort make this informa-tion part of the sign-up form. Send the customer a birthday card and make them a special offer to say thank you for their business.

Customers in this instance can be anyone from regular clientele right through to the chief executive officer at a company that you supply. Take the time to handwrite the card. Don't make it look mass produced. Be genuine in your comments but not overly personal if you don't know the person very well.

## Ask your customers for referrals

Referrals are simply when you ask an existing customer for the name of someone who they know who may be able to use your services or products. The main idea of a referral is that you contact the person being referred and tell them that your customer recommended that you call them.

It is the same as having someone on the inside. By mentioning the friend's or customer's name as a recommendation you automatically have your foot in the door. Referrals are a great way to generate new business.

Establishing a system where your current clients can provide you with the name of a friend or colleague who may be interested in your product or service is a very inexpensive way to generate extra business. It is a good idea to offer some form of reward for customers who offer referrals, such as a free product or a free service.

Many quality businesses receive a large proportion of their business from customer referrals. It is important that you feel confident enough to ask your customers for referrals—if they are happy with the work that you have done why wouldn't they be happy to pass on a lead to a new customer? You may be surprised at how willing people are to help you promote your business.

As a normal business practice it is a good idea to talk to the customer after all work is completed to make certain that they are 100 per cent satisfied. This is the perfect time to ask for the referral and also to really make certain that they are completely happy with the work that you have done.

Always be up-front and honest. I have often told my customers when I am going through a quiet time and I need some more work. All of a sudden I have a team of sales reps chasing business for me. I always find this very humbling and ring to say thank you for their help. There are a lot of cynical people in the world but I do believe that the majority of people will go out of their way to help others. In return for this I will always give 100 per cent for people who helped me in the past.

Don't be afraid to ask your customers to suggest some referrals for your business.

Say thank you to generate more business

A point that I have emphasised in this book is the impor-tance of telling customers that you appreciate them. A very easy way to do this is to send your customers a 'thank you' certificate.

For a number of years I worked as a sales manager for a cruise ship company. Part of my job was to call on travel wholesalers in Asia and America. Any business we received was a bonus because we were starting from scratch. Our management were very appreciative of the confidence that these companies were showing in us by sending their customers on our vessels.

To say 'thank you' a series of plaques was developed and sent to the various companies as they reached certain targets. We sent a thank you certificate for their first booking and as the business grew the plaques became less frequent but more valuable.

Every business has customers that spend a lot and those that spend a little. Work out a budget to suit your business and make up some form of thank you certificate. It may be something as simple as a letter to the company or it may be an unusual plaque that represents the type of business you operate.

# Chapter Three

## Jewish Wisdom for Business Success

There's a new thirst, a new quest for understanding people and talent in the workplace more than there was in previous decades.

You have to stay relevant and constantly challenge yourself to understand what's happening in the economy and in the business world in order to differentiate yourself and to really make a difference for your clients. You have to be real, open and authentic, and work with your clients in partnership — you can't try to sell nirvana to people.

You also can't have one customer if you plan to partner with a specific client for life because of high turnover rates. You have to have many relationships — have an extra foot in the door — within organizations to stay in it.

Technology changes and advances rapidly virtually every day of the year. New things are being discovered all the time, and the demands of the market shift regularly for a wide variety of reasons, not just economically.

## Jewish Wisdom for Business Success

Midrashim were handed down orally from generation to generation and only written down many centuries later. Typically, a midrash is a sophisticated commentary that sheds light on one of the deeper issues raised by a passage from the Torah.

In this case, the midrash takes the form of a story about the argument among the newly emancipated Israelites as they stood before the Sea of Reeds (which is often mistakenly translated in English versions of the Torah as the Red Sea). They were caught between the chasing Egyptian soldiers and the deep waters. As you can imagine, they were very afraid.

Fear, in fact, drove them towards recommending four modes of action that would have been disastrous. The midrash goes on to discuss these four faces of fear: self-sabotage, fight, retreat, and learned helplessness. Moses's response, found in the Torah, shows timeless wisdom for overcoming these four impulses. He doesn't just anticipate Nike's advertising slogan and tell the Israelites to "Just Do It!" He accepts the source of their fear and tells them how to overcome it. In doing so, he creates a template that anyone can use in any situation where fear is present. That template is so effective that it needs no updating—even three-and-a-half thousand years after Moses created it.

Pharaoh's lead horse was now clearly visible and the sun glinted off his raised sword. The people fell silent and looked at Moses. He had guided them this far. Moses looked out upon his people and uttered perhaps the most important words he would ever speak like a leader.

## Nothing Stands Before the Will

Motivation isn't just an asset that is useful in achieving success—it's a prerequisite. Without motivation, failure is guaran-teed. But how do people motivate themselves towards success? Most advice reverts to old clichés like "Knuckle down and bear it," "Put your nose to the grindstone," and "Hard work conquers all." While these nuggets of wisdom do contain kernels of truth, we can all cite examples in our own lives where they simply did not work. If you have built your own business you know that to succeed, you need to be a self-starter. For that, pure determination and endurance are not enough. Something else is required to reach your goal—and that is passion.

## Becoming the Rocket Man

This is what he had wanted to do ever since he was a boy in South Africa. As the countdown proceeded, his mind focused on the image. The rocket was his baby; he had paid for it with his money and he had managed the elaborate process of designing it and building it. But now it was time for launching it. One of his employees was actually going to push the button. It was Musk's turn to watch.

- **INSIGHT FOR BUSINESS:** Having a high position that demands respect doesn't mean that you are realizing your inner will. Never forget what makes you passionate, and work towards spending time doing it. Active reflection about yourself will help you keep in touch with your inner will. Magically, it also helps you perform the tasks of the outer will that are necessary in order to achieve the goals of the inner will.

- **INSIGHT FOR LIFE:** Recognize the differences between your inner will and your outer will. If you are staying true to your inner will (such as having a happy and fulfilling marriage), the acts of the outer will (such as remembering to take out the garbage), be-come so much easier to perform.

## Discovering Your Inner Will

To enjoy your business life or career and remain motivated to continue with it, the inner will must always be the focus of your attention. But for many of us, the question is what the inner and authentic will really is. How can we know what we are really passionate about? According to the Kabbalists, it is a soul thing: we are passionate about things that are closest to our authentic self. Unfortunately, many people have disguised their authentic self to such a degree that they no longer recognize that it exists. So the first and most important thing to do is to get in touch with it. This is easier said than done, but it is vital if real and sustained success is ever to be achieved.

The first thing to do is to become aware that the authentic self really does exist. Once you have acknowledged this, you are halfway

## Nothing Stands Before the Will

The second thing to do is to realize that the authentic self does not always follow logic. This does not mean that you cannot find a logical reason for what the authentic inner desire expresses. You usually can. However, the basis of the expression of your authentic and inner will and desire is not intellect or logic—it is pure soul-speak.

The expression of the authentic self can be exemplified by the love a parent has for a child. This love is not dependent on anything else. In most cases, it will always be there. Even

when the child may act in a way that is hurtful to the parent, the parent still feels love for the child, because that child is their flesh and blood, and the love is not based on any benefit they derive from the relationship with the child. The parent-child relationship is a quintessential bond that transcends any intellectual reason. In a similar vein, an expression of our authentic self cannot necessarily be logically explained. Very often we feel that we want something but the reason for it is not im-mediately apparent. This may be because we have just experienced and expressed our authentic self.

## Chapter Four

## Make The Most Of The Customers You Have

I once received a thank you gift from an accountant. It was a calculator with really big buttons. The firm's name was on the calculator with a message saying 'We appreciate your business'. The accompanying letter explained that, like the 'easy-to-use' calculator, they wanted to provide a service to my business that was 'easy to use'. I thought that this was very clever and I have remembered it for years.

We recently conducted a large survey of departing tour-ists at an international airport. It was a complicated project that involved a lot of communicating between our business and the airport management. The representative from the airport was very professional and helpful. This lady's assis-tance made the project run smoothly and successfully.

After the project was completed we sent a bunch of flowers and note expressing our sincere gratitude for the assistance that we had received.

This is something we always do. If someone goes out of their way to help us we like to go out of our way to thank them. Often we will send a letter to their boss explaining how a particular person went above and beyond the call of duty to assist us with a particular project.

We are always sincere in our praise and we only do it if the person has really been helpful. What we have found is that whenever we deal with the same person again they always go out of their way to help. We also generate a lot of business by doing this because the person that we have said thank you to tells everyone that we are a great company to deal with. Everyone wins.

Saying 'thank you' can take many different shapes. We recently purchased $200 dollars worth of damper for a promotion we were running. To say 'thank you' the baker gave us a huge loaf of crusty Italian bread. Now this was only a small gift on their behalf but we appreciated it and remembered their gesture enough to write about it in this book. Now we buy all of our bread from this baker.

You decide how best to thank your customers and business associates. They will take notice and you will benefit with extra business and word-of-mouth advertising that costs very little.

How many handwritten thank you notes do you receive in the post every day? If your letterbox is like mine I would guess that the answer is zero. People don't write thank you notes, but they should.

Buy some stamps, a bundle of postcards or greeting cards from the local newsagency and start writing. The response is instant and somewhat overwhelming. Showing that you appreciate your customers and their business is an important step in keeping the business for a long time.

One of the most successful car salespeople in the United States used to spend more on cards and postage every year than most of his colleagues earned. He used to sell between five and six vehicles every day of the week and most of his customers spent their lives buying cars from him. He sent birthday cards, thank you cards, Christmas cards, the lot. What he ended up with was a loyal client base that were his friends as well as his customers.

## What Is A Loyalty Program And Can You Use One?

In simple terms a loyalty program is a structured way of giving a benefit to customers who use your business regularly. The aim is to make the rewards appealing enough so the customers will not use the opposition because they are trying to achieve some type

of prize you are offering. The most famous loyalty programs are the ones run by the airlines— frequent flier campaigns. This does not mean they only work for large companies.

This business had about 100 children attending classes on a weekly basis. The cost for tutoring in two subjects amounted to $20 per month per student. As with many small businesses, the lady operating this one started with minimal capital and no marketing expertise but she man-aged to build it up to a good size. However, it was proving difficult to break the 100 student barrier and get into her profit-making zone.

After taking a close look at the business and considering that the budget for marketing was very minimal, the best source of potential customers seemed to be with the existing parents. Based on 100 students it was fair to assume that this provided a pool of about 175 parents (taking into account single-parent families and multiple children in the one family).

A flyer was made on the company PC introducing the loyalty program. Basically, as students reached a milestone, such as three months, six months or twelve months, they received one month's free tutoring—the children probably did not care less about this but the parents did and they were the ones that signed the cheques.

Further to this the parents were given certificates to give to their friends and colleagues offering free academic testing for children. This initiative was used to encourage the friend or colleague to take their child along and be tested to assess their current academic level. If they decided to sign their children up for some coaching the referring parent received a free month's tuition for their own child. Smart parents found plenty of friends

and received up to a year of free tutoring simply by referring other people to the coaching company in an easy and clear way.

This principle can be applied to virtually every business. If you have customers staying with you for a long time, reward them—they are your best form of advertising. Taking customers for granted is one of the greatest business tragedies.

Loyalty programs and incentives work exceptionally well. Take your time, plan it properly and follow it through. Talk to your customers about your idea; they will tell you what will motivate them to spend more with your business.

Many businesses, particularly restaurants, offer loyalty cards where regular customers receive a 10 per cent dis-count. Every time my wife and I go to our local Chinese restaurant, the owner, Mr Wong, hands us the bill with a 10 per cent discount. I always tell him that he doesn't have to do this but he insists. He states that we eat at his restaurant once per week and we tell lots of our friends how good his food is. He laughs and says that we generate half of his business making it well worth his 10 per cent discount.

Another idea I discovered and thought was very clever was with a local commercial cleaning company. Every year they offered to clean the houses of five staff members from their largest customers. These customers awarded the house cleaning as a prize for their staff members and basically everyone was happy. The cleaners had cemented their relationship with their clients. The clients had rewarded a few members of their team with a thank you prize and the staff members themselves had clean houses.

All businesses can benefit from rewarding customers for being loyal. The hard part is to determine how you can best reward your particular customers.

www.ingramcontent.com/pod-product-compliance
Lightning Source LLC
Chambersburg PA
CBHW080440220526
45465CB00009B/3360